101 Cool

MW00891361

in Madrid

Introduction

So you're going to Madrid, huh? You lucky lucky thing! You are sure in for a treat because Madrid is truly one of the most magical cities on this planet. There's a mix of incredible architecture, awesome restaurants and cafes, and amazing nightlife and shopping that makes Madrid one of the most enduringly popular tourist destinations on the face of the earth.

In this guide, we'll be giving you the low down on:
- the very best things to shove in your pie hole, from street food staples like calamari sandwiches to Michelin star restaurants
- the best shopping so that you can take a little piece of Madrid back home with you
- incredible festivals, whether you're into local flamenco dancing on you want to rock out to indie bands
- the coolest historical and cultural sights that you simply cannot afford to miss
- where to party like someone from Madrid and make local friends
- and tonnes more coolness besides!

Let's not waste any more time – here are the 101 coolest things not to miss in Madrid!

1. Feast on Calamari Sandwiches

One thing that's a guarantee on your trip to Madrid is that you will eat exceptionally well. And the nice thing about Madrid is that it doesn't matter what your budget is, you'll find some incredible food to match your wallet regardless. And if you are looking for cheap eats, you can't do much better than the delicious calamari sandwiches that can be found across the city. The calamari is breaded, fried, and placed inside a fluffy bread roll. Ideal hangover food, and a restaurant called La Ideal is said to serve up the best calamari sandwiches in the city.

2. Hop Bar to Bar, Tapa to Tapa

When in Madrid, it's a great idea to eat and drink just like the locals do. Instead of filling yourself up with a heavy dinner, the best way to eat and drink in the early evening is by hopping from bar to bar and nibbling on plates of tapas as you go. The tapas is not something you ordinarily have to pay extra for, it actually comes with your 1 euro glass of beer. You could find yourself munching on crunchy chicharron (pork rinds), a cooling bowl of gazpacho, or a melt in the mouth slice of Spanish tortilla.

3. Immerse Yourself in Art at the Museo Del Prado

To say that there is a vibrant arts culture in Madrid is an understatement. This city is a major player on the global stage when it comes to the arts, and the most acclaimed gallery in the city is Museo del Prado. The collection of European art here is simply one of the finest in Europe with over 7600 paintings, 4800 prints, 8000 drawings, and 1000 sculptures. Works from the likes of Goya, Valezquez, and Rembrandt, amongst many others are in the permanent collection. An absolute must for art lovers.

4. Indulge in Oysters and Cocktails at The Urban

The Urban is a 5* hotel in the centre of Madrid that will promise you an unforgettable stay if your budget stretches that far. But if not, no worries, because The Urban has its very own Glass Bar where everyone is welcome as long as they are dressed appropriately. This is the perfect place to spend a special evening on a romantic trip. They serve fresh oysters and their cocktail menu is second to none.

5. Take a Cable Car Trip Over the City

Madrid is a stunning city, but there aren't a huge number of high buildings from which you can take in the whole panorama of the Spanish capital. If you are looking for a view to die for, all you need to do is take a ride on the Telerifico, which is a cable car system in Madrid. A ride on the cable car will take you above the city's impressive parks, the Manzaneres river, and you'll get to see major sights like the Temple of Debod and Plaza Espana from a great height. The Telerifico only runs from April to September so this is one for summertime visitors.

6. Go Boating on the Lake at Retiro Park

Retiro Park is simply one of the most beautiful parks in the world, and when you feel as though you need a little respite from cars, noise, and endless tapas, this is a great place to relax and unwind. One of the most popular features of the park is the large boating lake. This is a perfect Sunday activity for when the museums are closed and you want to snuggle up to your loved one with a romantic boating trip.

7. Find a Bargain at El Rastro Flea Market

El Rastro is a Madrid institution. Every Sunday, this open air market attracts thousands of visitors along Plaza de Cascorro.

The space is truly gargantuan, and over 3500 stalls can be held here every week, which is fantastic news for bargain hunters on a trip to Madrid. At El Rastro, you can find all kinds of goodies, from vintage furniture through to hand made pieces of jewellery. Just be sure to have Google Maps switched on because it's all too easy to get lost!

8. Chow Down on Churros at San Gines

Got a sweet tooth? You're in luck because so do the Madrid locals, but when they need a sugar fix, they do one better than grabbing a bar of chocolate from their local shop. To satisfy their sugar cravings, they indulge in sugar coated churros dipped in chocolate. Churros are essentially long donuts covered in sugar, and the locals will dip this into a freshly made thick hot chocolate. You'll be able to find a decadent plate of churros in many places across the city but San Gines is widely regarded as the ultimate churros destination.

9. Have Your Photo Taken With The Bear and The Strawberry Tree

As you walk along the pretty streets of the city, you'll notice more than a sprinkling of statues. One that stands out is of a bear and a strawberry tree. This iconic installation is the work of Antonio Navarro Santafé, and it was constructed in 1967. The reason for a bear and a strawberry tree is because these two symbols appear on the Madrid coat of arms. This is the perfect place for a selfie with your loved ones!

10. Party Hard at Kapital

Love to party hard? So do the local people from Madrid, often until daylight breaks! This means that you will have ample opportunity to drink and dance until the early hours on your trip. But when you're new to a city, knowing the best place to go for a good time is tricky. Fortunately, you can't go far wrong with a night out at Kapital, one of the most renowned clubs in the city. There are seven floors of pumping music, so if the hip-hop room isn't doing it for you, you could see if the salsa room is more up your alley.

11. Take in a Traditional Zarzuela Performance

Almost everybody around the world has heard about Spanish flamenco dancing, but what about zarzuela? This form of Spanish performance isn't quite so celebrated, but it's well worth catching a show on your visit to Madrid, and the impressive Teatro de Zarzuela is the place to do so. Zarzuela is a type of musical theatre that switches between spoken and sung scenes. While the lyrics will be in Spanish, it's worth visiting for the stunning visuals and the atmosphere alone. There are also contemporary dance performances at the Teatro de Zarzuela if that is more your thing.

12. Find Unique Objects at Mercado Central de Diseno

Looking for something extra cool to act as a permanent reminder of the days you have spent in Madrid? Well, there is bound to be something that catches your eye at the impressive Mercado Central de Diseno. This outdoor market brings together around 150 designers, who specialise in everything from funky clothes and jewellery to hand made glassware so that you can find that one special item. There's also food and drink on offer, including the famous fried calamari sandwiches of Madrid.

13. Eat Paella All Day Long

When you envisage yourself in Madrid, you might imagine yourself tucking into a piping hot bowl of paella for every meal, and quite honestly, that could be a reality! While this dish isn't actually from Madrid but from Valencia, it is popular all over Spain and you will see it on virtually every menu you can find in the capital. If you've never tried paella before, it's a traditional rice dish, combined with saffron, seafood, chicken, peas, and lots and lots of olive oil. For a truly exceptional plate of paella, head to Casa Benigna where the paella is nothing short of outstanding.

14. Rock out at DCode Festival

Every September, Madrid rocks out like no other city in Europe. That's because the incredible and raucous Dcode Festival lands in the city and takes over a huge space where over 25,000 people join in with the fun on a university campus. This rock and indie festival attracts some of the biggest names in music, including Foals, Beck, Suede, and Bombay Bicycle Club. If you're a rock music fan, it's worth making the trip for this festival alone.

15. Get Beer Happy at Madrid Beer Week

The locals in Madrid sure do love a glass of cold beer. And the levels of beer appreciation seriously escalate during Madrid Beer Week, which takes place during June each year. Tonnes of beer makers and microbreweries from Madrid and right across Spain come to together to offer tastings, beer and food pairings, "meet the maker" sessions, and tonnes more beer centred fun besides.

16. Get Back to Nature at Madrid Zoo

If you love animals, you can do one better than petting stray cats that roam the streets of Madrid at night. Madrid Zoo covers 20 hectares in the Caso de Campo park, and as it opened in 1770, it is one of the oldest zoos on the planet. This is one of the few zoos in the world that houses giant pandas, and seeing them happily munching on bamboo is a really special treat. There is also a petting zoo, a dolphin exhibit, an aviary, and a train and boat tour.

17. Take in a Free Movie at Cineteca Madrid

Amidst all of your sightseeing, there might be a time when you simply want to kick back with a good movie. Cineteca, a cultural centre in Madrid is the place to do so. They err on the side of documentaries, and most of the screenings here are free, so this is also the ideal place to save your pennies. There are also cultural activities such as exhibition openings, performances, and lectures, as well as a rather lovely restaurant and bar that serves up local beers from Madrid.

18. Hang out With Madrid's Hipsters at Cazador Bar

Fancy yourself as a bit of a hipster, or perhaps you just want to make friends with Madrid's trendy set? If that sounds like you, waste no time and head to Bar Cazador in the evening. This is officially a gay bar but it's very straight friendly, and this is where you'll find that many of the creative types (artists, photographers, writers, and fashion designers) hang out over a glass of beer or a cocktail. This place really fills up over the weekend, so arrive early for a table if you want to be more comfortable.

19. Hit the Ski Slopes at Valdesqui

When you think of Madrid, you probably don't think of it as a ski destination. Sure, it's not the Swiss Alps, but if you've ever visited the Spanish capital in the winter months, you'll know how chilly it can get, and there are mountain ranges just outside of the city. In fact, Valdesqui, a ski range in the Guadarrama mountain range is just about an hour's drive from Madrid. There are 29 pistes of varying difficulties so that complete beginners to advanced skiers can enjoy the slopes.

20. Watch Spring Bloom at La Quinta de Los Molinos

For park lovers, Madrid is the ideal city getaway in Europe. There are so many parks, in fact, that many of them are not even known by locals, and one of the hidden gems is La Quinta de Los Molinos. This park is at its very best at the beginning of springtime in March. The park is littered with an abundance of beautiful almond trees, and each March, these trees blossom with pink and white flowers, which both look and smell beautiful.

21. Join in the San Isidro Celebrations

May 15th is a very special day on the Madrid calendar, the day of San Isidro. To celebrate the life of this saint, the weekend of the Saint's Day is a riot of celebrations. This is the time when you will get to see all the traditions of Madrid on the streets. There will be parades full of people and colours, live music playing from every corner, and people will enjoy eating the most traditional dishes. You will also see people dancing the traditional "choti" dance in pairs. What's more, most of the festivities and activities are totally free.

22. Get Festive at the Christmas Market in Plaza Mayor

Spain is often thought of as a summertime destination, and while there is no doubt that it can be great to take in some of that Spanish heat during the summer months, Madrid is also spectacular in the run up to Christmas. In the Plaza Mayor, which is the main square in the city, a festive market takes over the whole space for most of December. You'll have the opportunity to purchase unique Christmas gifts, chow down on festive culinary treats, and feel the atmosphere of Christmas with all the decorations surrounding you.

23. Learn About Spanish Impressionism at the Sorolla Museum

If you love nothing more than to hop from museum to museum, you're in luck because the Spanish capital has a museum culture that can rival any city in the world. One smaller museum that you absolutely shouldn't miss is the Sorolla Museum. The museum features the work of the

Spanish impressionist painter, Joaquin Sorolla. Originally the house of the artist, it was converted into a museum after the death of his widow in 1962. As well as a place to view the artist's paintings, it's a place to see where and how the artist worked, painted, and lived his life.

24. Fill Up Your Stomach With Delicious Cocido

If you're visiting Madrid during the winter time, you'll want something to warm your bones from the inside out, and a heaped bowl of cocido will do just the trick. Cocido is a chickpea and meat stew local to Madrid, that can include blood sausage, pork sausage, lard, bacon, and other meat offcuts. It can also feature potatoes, carrots, and green beans. We guarantee that it's the most delicious peasant stew that you will ever taste.

25. Discover Ancient History at the National Archaeological Museum of Spain

Established in 1867, the National Archaeology Museum of Spain is one of the world's premiere places to look at archaeological artefacts and learn about ancient history. The museum contains a staggering number of different objects.

You'll get to see all kinds of artefacts from Ancient Islamic Spain, Ancient Egypt, Greek, Roman, Celtic periods, and much more besides. It's possible to spend more than a day exploring the collection, so take your time with it!

26. Take a Street Art Tour

In order to really understand a city, it's important to get beyond what exists behind glass containers in museums, and actually feel the lifeblood of a city on the streets. A way of appreciating Madrid's artistic counterculture is by paying attention to the art that is painted on to the city's walls. You are most likely to see Madrid's street art in the outer suburbs of the city, and it's a great idea to take a guided street art tour so that you can really appreciate the political messages and the creative skill that go into the wall murals you might otherwise walk right past.

27. Sample Spanish Delicacies at Mercado de San Miguel

If you think of yourself as a bit of a foodie, there is one market that will totally bowl you over: Mercado de San Miguel in the centre of the city. The market structure of iron and glass is spectacular enough in its own right, but when you venture inside and start tasting the amazingness on offer, you'll want to stay inside all day. There are more than 30 carefully selected vendors, selling products such as authentic Spanish cheeses, olives, cured meats, and wines and cocktails. The vendors are also very eager to hand out free samples!

28. Feel Madrid's Creativity at Nomada Market

As a European capital city, Madrid has a burgeoning creative streak. As a visitor it can be hard to discover the underground creativity of a place, but when you visit Madrid it's easy – just head to the Nomada Market. The Nomada Market is essentially an independent design fair that gives independent creators who aren't backed by major corporations the chance to showcase their wares. If you want to take something exciting, innovative and original home with you, this is the place. You'll be able to find ceramics, glassware, fashion, jewellery, and much more.

29. Brush Up Your Spanish Skills

Was the last time that you spoke Spanish in high school? If so, it might be time to brush up your Spanish skills, because there is surprisingly little English spoken on the streets of

Madrid and you could find yourself in a sticky situation if you aren't at least familiar with some language basics. And if you are sticking around for a while, it can be a great idea to actually enrol in Spanish School, and there are numerous of these in Madrid that allow you to study for as little as a week. Your Madrid experience will be 100% richer if you can actually converse with the locals!

30. Join in With Madrid's Gay Pride Festivities

Madrid is one of the most gay friendly cities in the world, and this is never more evident than during the Gay Pride celebrations that occur at the end of June or beginning of July each year. There are tonnes of parties in the city's happening gay clubs, but the highlight has to be the main parade, with hundreds of floats that navigate their way through the city streets as merry makes cheer them on and wave their rainbow flags with pride. Why not be a part of the celebrations?

31. Take a Swim at Parque Deportivo Puerta del Hierro

Summertime in Madrid is hot – like, seriously hot. If you are visiting during the summer months and you are desperate for a way to escape the bustling streets and need to cool down, you should look no further than the Parque Deportivo Puerta del Hierro. There is lots of space here to relax and play sports, but the park is most well known for its Olympic size swimming pool. Whether you just want to splash around and feel the cool water on you or do some serious laps, this is the place.

32. Enjoy Lunch With a View at Café del Rio

Are you looking for somewhere that serves up tasty Spanish grub and that also offers a killer view? Café del Rio is the perfect spot. As you might have gleaned by the name, it's right on the river side, and from the upper terrace, you'll have a majestic view of the gorgeous Royal Palace on the other side. But this isn't the kind of place that offers a view and disappointing food. Not even close. Be sure to try the oxtail puff pastry, the black rice with calamari, and the Bluefin tuna. You'll have zero regrets.

33. Warm Yourself by the Fire at El Patio Del Fisgon

The Salamanca district is one of the trendiest neighbourhoods in the city, and El Patio del Fisgon is a hidden gem where you'll want to spend plenty of time after days of sightseeing and shopping. The best thing about this restaurant-bar is its stunning outdoor terrace. And while most outdoor terraces in Madrid can only be used in the spring and summer months, that's not the case with El Patio del Fisgon. A stunning fireplace will warm up your bones no matter the time of year, so you can enjoy your outdoor cocktail even if you're visiting in the winter.

34. Visit an Authentic Spanish Bar: Fatigas del Querer

There is absolutely no shortage of places for an evening drink in Madrid, but when you aren't a local, it can be hard to know the best places to go. Trust us when we say that Fatigas del Querer is a local bar that is packed full of charm, and that it should be at the very top of your bar hit-list. The staff are extremely friendly, the wine is delicious, and the food is great quality and plentiful (don't leave before you try their blood sausage). You'll be back again and again!

35. Go Designer Shopping in Salamanca

If you are looking for the trendiest spots in Madrid, you need to base yourself in the Salamanca neighbourhood. This is the place where you can find all of the Spanish designer stores, and you'll also find independent boutiques. It's on Calle Serrano that you'll find upmarket department stores where you can find anything your heart desires, and on Calle Claudio Coello you'll be immersed in a shopping street with some of the more up-and-coming designers.

36. Have a Local Experience With Couchsurfing

Yes, staying in a lovely hotel can be a great way to pass your days in Madrid, and a hostel dorm can be great for connecting with other travellers like yourself, but neither of these accommodation options really gives you a taste of how people from Madrid truly live. Couchsurfing.com is a website that puts you in touch with local people, and you can stay on their spare couch or bed for free. As well as a great money saving exercise, this is a fantastic way to have an authentic cultural exchange.

37. Take a Day Trip to El Escorial

If you have filled your boots with sightseeing inside Madrid and you are looking for a little bit of tranquillity, El Escorial makes for a great day trip as it's less than an hour away. El Escorial is a historic residence of the King of Spain, and it functions as a royal palace, a museum, a school, and a convent all in one. With so much to see and explore, it's more than possible to spend the entire day here and really immerse yourself in the stunning Spanish gothic architecture of the buildings.

38. Be Wowed by the Royal Palace of Madrid

The official residence of the Spanish Royal family, the Royal Palace of Madrid is arguably the most important building in the entire country. The palace dates back to the latter half of the 18th century, and with a staggering 3418 rooms, this is the largest Royal Palace in all of Europe. The palace is impressive enough from the outside, but it's also possible to enter and walk around its hallways and rooms where you'll be able to spot artworks from Caravaggio, Valezquez, Goya, and many other prominent European artists. Don't miss the Royal Armoury, which contains one of the most comprehensive armoury collections in the world, with pieces dating back to the 13th century.

39. Cool Down With an Ice Cream From Sienna

The summertime in Madrid can be seriously hot. So hot that you might be grasping for gelato after gelato. And who could blame you with the number of incredible ice cream parlours in the city? One of the very best is Sienna. At Sienna, they follow Italian recipes to the ice cream is creamy and silky smooth, and there's an assortment of wonderful flavours, from the traditional to more creative options. The salted caramel is said to be particularly special. And because Sienna is open until past midnight, you could even pop out of your hotel room for a late night ice cream jaunt – sometimes you just have to!

40. Take an Art Class at Estudio de Arte

Spain is a country full of artists, but instead of walking from museum to museum, why not give Valezquez a run for his money and pick up a paintbrush yourself? At the Estudio de Arte, you can take classes in drawing, painting, print making, restoration, and clay work. There are classes for kids and adults, so let your creative streak run wild!

41. Drink Coffee With the Locals at Café de Ruiz

Do you want to relax and take a coffee where the locals take their coffee and away from the bustle of the main square?

Café de Ruiz is the place to do so. Located a little north of the main centre, this is the place to grab a really high quality espresso, sit back in a comfortable sofa, and feel perfectly at home. They also make their own ice cream on site, so if you have a sweet tooth, be sure to indulge.

42. Enjoy Truly Decadent Cocktails at Tatel

If you love nothing more than to indulge in a cocktail or two, Madrid is the city for you. There are many cocktail bars dotted around the city, but one that you absolutely can't afford to miss is Tatel in the Salamanca neighbourhood. There are many innovative cocktails available, and one of the best is a port cocktail made from port, spiced rum, date syrup, and a whole egg. It's a decadent choice to say the least.

43. Visit an Egyptian Temple in Madrid

A temple from Ancient Egypt in the centre of Madrid? Yup! Unlikely as it may seem, the Temple of Debod was a temple from Egypt that was dismantled and then put back together in the Spanish capital city. The temple dates right back to 200 BC, and was dedicated to the Goddess Isis. After the construction of the Aswan High Dam, the reservoir posed a threat to the temple, and it was consequently gifted to Madrid, and it now sits in the Parque del Oeste.

44. Enjoy a Drink With a View at Circulo de Bellas Artes

Madrid is a stunning city, but you can only comprehend a fraction of its beauty from the streets. For the best view of the city, be sure to scale the Circulo de Bellas Artes where there is a café and bar on the rooftop that offers a jaw dropping panorama of the whole city. It costs a few euros to actually enter, but it's well worth the cost for the photo opportunities alone. Sit and relax with a coffee or a cocktail, and you'll feel as though you're on top of the world.

45. Look at Picasso's Guernica Up Close

There are a few paintings in the world that everyone has stored in the recess of the brain, whether they are an art fan or not. Picasso's Guernica, a painting that depicts an anti-war sentiment following the bombing of Guernica, is one such painting. Prints and reproductions of the painting can be found right across the globe, but there is only one place where you can see the real deal, and that's at the Museo Reina Sofia in Madrid.

46. Be Wowed by the Basilica de San Francisco El Grande

Something that keeps tourists flocking to Madrid year after year is the stunning religious architecture, and if you want to get your fill of beautiful churches while you are in the city, be sure to start with the Basilica de San Francisco El Grande. This baroque church has an extraordinary frescoed dome, which happens to be the largest in Spain and the fourth largest in the world. The central fresco was painted by a young Goya, and you can even spot a self portrait of Goya within the fresco itself.

47. Indulge in Michelin Star Food at Al Trapo

Madrid has no less than nine Michelin star restaurants, and one that is enduringly popular with both critics and diners alike is Al Trapo in the city centre. This place is definitely at the cutting edge of Spanish dining, but it doesn't feel stuffy at all. The pork cheeks are a Spanish favourite that people who want a local taste of Madrid will enjoy, while the marinated anchovies in red curry sauce is more of an "out there" choice for food adventurers.

48. Walk Through an Open-Air Sculpture Museum

In Madrid, you don't have to make a compromise between spending time enjoying outdoor activities and soaking up as much culture as possible because there is an incredible open-air sculpture museum in the city. The sculpture museum is a retrospective of work from the 1930s to the present day, with 17 different sculptures from 17 different Spanish artists.

49. Eat in the World's Oldest Restaurant!

There are endless opportunities for great dining in the Spanish capital, but one of the most special of them all has to be Restaurant Botin. Why is this place such a must visit restaurant? Because it's officially the oldest restaurant in the world according the Guinness World Records. Restaurant Botin first opened its doors in 1725, which is almost 300 years ago! Since then, it has been serving up traditional Spanish dishes to hungry locals, and you won't want to miss their roast suckling pig.

50. Go Vintage Shopping at Pepita is Dead

Want to do a spot of shopping while you're in Madrid but aren't sure where to start? Of course, Madrid is home to designer and high street stores, but for clothing that's way more unique, head to Pepita is Dead, a vintage clothing store in the centre of Madrid. The clothing is very carefully selected, and everything is dated between 1950 and 1990 so you'll know that you'll be buying something authentically vintage. They stock menswear, womenswear, and clothes for kids as well.

51. Share a Big Jug of Sangria!

While Spanish red wine is delicious, if you visit Madrid in the summer months, you might be looking for a drink that is a little lighter and fresher. In steps sangria, the ultimate Spanish summer drink, a mixture of red wine, fruit, orange juice, and sometimes a little bit of soda water. Sangria is best consumed with friends, in a big jug, on a shaded terrace. For something a little different, head to Restaurant Ojala, where their white sangria (made with white wine) is the highlight of the drinks menu.

52. Wallow in Nature at Madrid's Botanical Gardens

Because the Prado Museum is one of the most impressive art galleries in the world, many people neglect to take time and appreciate the 8 hectare botanical garden that's located right in front of the museum. But if you are looking for a spot of peace after rubbing shoulders with so many tourists in the museum, this extraordinary garden is a place to chill. The garden was founded in the mid 18th century by King Ferdinand VI, and it contains more than 30,000 plants and 1500 trees. The garden also contains the largest herbarium in all of Spain.

53. Take Home Handmade Souvenirs at El Arco Artesania

When it comes to souvenir shopping, you'll want to avoid most of the places with branded mugs and tacky t-shirts. But for something authentic, original, and handmade, waste no time and head straight to El Arco Artesania, which is located in the south-west corner of the Plaza Mayor. In this shop, everything is made by hand, and you'll be able to find stoneware, ceramics, glassware, things for your home, jewellery, beautiful papier-mache figures, and lots more – you'll be spoiled for choice!

54. Explore Spanish Ceramics at Antigua Casa Talavera

When you walk past the beautiful tiled façade of this old ceramics shop in the centre of Madrid, you know that you are in for a treat. Inside, it's even more magical. You won't find anything mass produced in this small ceramics seller, but hand made items from Andalucia and Toledo. If you need to do some souvenir shopping, this is the place to get it done. Whether you walk away with a water jug or a whole new set of kitchen crockery, you'll be leaving Madrid with something that's extra special.

55. Eat the Most Exclusive Sandwich of Your Life

A sandwich is a sandwich is a sandwich, right? Wrong. At Bocadilleria Clandestina, sandwiches are super exclusive. This is an underground sandwich joint, and everybody needs a password to enter. Are the sandwiches worth it? Too right they are. You could try the sandwich with panko crusted shrimp and dragon sauce, or perhaps the quinoa fillets with horseradish mayo on carrot bread is more your thing. Each sandwich comes with a beer for 7 euros, which isn't bad for the best sandwich of your life. Contact them and book a table to get the magic password.

56. Get Physical With a Day Hike at La Pedriza

Are you the kind of person who is less into sightseeing and more into actually doing stuff? In that case, it's a great idea to travel just 45 minutes outside of the centre of Madrid, where you'll be immersed in complete peace and tranquillity in the Guadarrama mountain range where the La Pedriza hill is located. This is a popular day hike for Madrid locals, and it isn't for the faint hearted. The trip up and down will take you a good eight hours, and it's steep, so be sure to pack a lunch and take plenty of water with you. The views at the top will be totally worth it!

57. Eat Spanish Tortilla Until You Burst

If there is one dish that everyone thinks of when they think of Spain it's Spanish tortilla or Spanish omelette. This is a simple dish that's basically a thick omelette loaded up with garlic, onion, lots of olive oil, sliced thin potatoes, and sometimes a touch of paprika as well. If you've never tried it before, now is your chance, because virtually everywhere that serves food in Madrid will sell this, from hole in the wall tapas joints to fancy restaurants. And it's delicious, so trust us when we say you should chow down on as much Spanish tortilla as is humanly possible.

58. Get to Grips with Village Life at Patones de Arriba

While Madrid is an exciting and dynamic city, if you have the urge to discover a slice of Spain that is a little more traditional and slower paced, you should absolutely take a day trip to Patones de Arriba. This is a village just 60km outside of the city, but it's a world away from the hustle and bustle of the Spanish capital. The village is said to be more than one thousand years old, and much of the architecture is slate, with an old, worn, but immensely charming feel. Walk the cobbled streets and pop into one of the bars for some tapas, and you'll feel instantly restored.

59. Visit an Annual Medieval Market

Just around 35 km outside of the city, lies the small town of Alcala de Henares. This isn't a town that's normally on the agenda of most visitors, but during one week in October, the town steps back in time, and a medieval market opens in the town square. During this Cervantes Week, there are gastronomic delights from the 16th and 17th century that you can sample, and there will be lots of live music, dancing, and theatre performances that will transport you back in time.

60. Watch an Art House Movie at Cines Capitol

Madrid is an awesome city for sightseeing and eating lots of yummy local food, but when you just want to spend an evening watching a good movie, Cines Capitol is the place to be. The cinema is located on the ground floor of a 15 storey art deco building, and the interior is beautifully opulent, with velvet curtains and seating. Cines Capitol is also dedicated to showcasing an exciting programme of art house films that you wouldn't see in your regular high street cinema.

61. Hit a few Golf Balls at Club de Campo

If your idea of a relaxing break is to unpack and then head to the nearest golf course, Madrid is the ideal city break location for you. There are numerous golf courses dotted around, and one of the most prestigious is the Club de Campo Villa de Madrid. It was founded in 1929, and it is considered to be one of the greatest courses in Madrid, and during its lifespan it has played host to many important competitions. The course is open to visitors from Monday to Thursday.

62. Cool Yourself Down With a Granizado

If you visit Madrid during the summertime, you'll definitely be looking for some ways to cool down. Take a look around you and you'll see that one of the most popular ways for locals to cope with the heat is by slurping on a granizado. A granizado is essentially the Spanish version of a slushy, and it can come in a variety of delicious flavours. If you are wondering where to grab one for yourself, head to one of the many ice cream parlours around the city.

63. Immerse Yourself in Spanish Dance at the Annual Flamenco Festival

What is more Spanish than a live flamenco show? Well, at the annual flamenco festival you won't just get to see one flamenco performance, but hundreds! The Suma Flamenco Festival takes over Madrid every June, and you will have the opportunity to watch flamenco shows, from the traditional to the innovative, in ten boroughs across the capital city. By the time you head home, you'll be a flamenco expert!

64. Explore Madrid's Urban Underside at Mulafest

Mulafest is one of the most unique festivals hosted in Madrid. This festival of "urban trends" comprises the likes of breakdance, open air concerts, skate boarding, tattoos, and car shows. This is the festival that really allows you to get to grips with countercultures that exist within the city, without having to trek around any seedy dive bars you really don't want to go to. It will also open you up to the incredible creativity and innovation of Madrid's youth. It takes place each year in June.

65. Listen to a Classical Concert at the Auditorio Nacional

Madrid is a wonderful place to soak up some culture. Once you are done with a day of looking at religious buildings and exploring museums, you can relax into a cultural evening of classical music at the Auditorio Nacional. It is the residence of both the National Orchestra of Spain and the Symphony Orchestra of Madrid, so you are practically guaranteed that any performance here will be world class.

66. Relax and Unwind in a Madrid Hammam

Madrid is the kind of city that you visit to have an awesome time with lots of drinking and eating and merriment, but if you need some space to relax, the city can offer that too. Hammam Al Andulus offers a total Arabian baths experience for people searching for some downtime. These baths are a candle lit oasis, perfect for soothing tired muscles. You can also indulge in one of the many massages or treatments on-site, and you can sip on refreshing mint tea.

67. Sip on Café con Leche in the Plaza Mayor

Madrid is a city full of charming plazas where you can sip on coffee, a glass of wine, and do a spot of shopping. But probably the most famous and iconic plaza of them all is Plaza Mayor. This square dates all the way back to the 16th century, having been built during the reign of Philip III. Although it's extraordinarily grand, very little has changed in the Plaza Mayor since those days. People even still live in residential buildings on the square. There are countless cafes here, so it's a great place to order a café con leche and watch the world go by.

68. Discover Ancient Madrid at the City Walls

As you walk around Madrid, you will find little signs of life in the city as it existed before the 18th century. That is until you visit the old city walls, which date back to the 11th century. Comprised of red limestone, granite, and brick, these walls were built by Alfonso VI following his capture of the Moors. He took Muslim Moors as prisoners and had them build the walls over the course of nine years.

69. Visit a Ghost Metro Station

There is one metro station in Madrid unlike any of the others, Estacion de Chamberi. The station is something of local legend because most Madrid locals have never had the opportunity to alight at this station. It did, in fact, close its doors in 1966, and the station now serves as a museum/installation that recreates the inauguration of the station in 1919. You'll be able to see old train posters from the time, ticket offices, and other fascinating memorabilia.

70. Indulge in a Big Bowl of Callos

Yes, there is yet more eating to do! You can't say that you have had the authentic Madrid experience until you have sat down with a steaming bowl of callos. This peasant dish may not be to everyone's tastes because the primary ingredient is tripe, but if you're down with offal, you are going to love it. The tripe is combined with chickpeas, blood sausage, chorizo, and a tomato and meat broth. It's the perfect dish for a winter's day, and it dates right back to the 15th century.

71. Discover Spanish Fashion and Costumes at Museo del Traje

As you walk around Madrid's streets, you can't fail to notice how chic the local population looks, but when you visit the Museo del Traje, you'll begin to appreciate the influence of Spanish fashion, clothing, and costumes across a much longer expanse of time. The collection here contains a staggering 160,000 items, with clothing from the Middle Ages right up to works from Spanish fashion designers creating garments today.

72. Usher in Autumn With the Festival de Otono

The summer months of Madrid can be swelteringly hot, and the locals can breathe a sigh of relief when autumn finally comes around. To celebrate the beginning of the autumn season, there is a month long festival dedicated to autumn during October. This is, at its heart, a cultural festival, and theatre companies, dance groups, orchestras, and musicians from all over the world are invited to play on some of Madrid's most celebrated stages during the month.

73. Chow Down on Pig's Ear

If you really want to eat like one of the locals on your trip to Madrid, there's one dish that you simply have to try at least once: pig's ear. And no, it's not a euphemism for something a little more delicate, we're literally talking about chowing down on the ear of a pig here. So the ear of a pig is fried, and sometimes onions and mushrooms are included as well. Wash it down with a cold glass of beer and you'll survive to tell the tale!

74. Discover Spanish Contemporary Art at The New Gallery

Madrid's arts culture is incredible, but it's not only the classic works of art that put Madrid on the global art map. There are also many young, practicing artists in the city, and there are tonnes of galleries where you can get to grips with the city's burgeoning contemporary art scene. One gallery that you shouldn't miss is The New Gallery. It has only been open since 2012, and the owners are dedicated to providing a platform for up and coming local artistic talent.

75. Relax in a Swiss Tea Room

Okay, so you may not expressly visit Madrid with the purpose of sipping on tea, but if you are a tea drinker and you feel overwhelmed by the amount of coffee around you in Madrid, make sure that you stop for a delicious cup of tea at Tekoe, a Swiss tea room. This is exactly the place to escape the mania of the city and to take it easy with one of their many different teas from around the world. They also hold tea tastings if you want to really explore the history, culture, and flavours of tea in Europe.

76. Watch Your Favourite Band at Costello Club

A night of live music is always a fun night out. You might not think that you'd get to see your favourite band on a trip to Madrid, but actually, the city has an incredible live music culture, and Costello Club is a venue where you just might get to see one of your favourite music acts perform. This is also a place where young, local people like to hang out, so if you want to make some new friends, this is the place to be.

Sometimes the acts even linger around a have a few drinks too.

77. Immerse Yourself in Fado at Madrid's Fado Festival

You would be forgiven for thinking for thinking that a Fado Festival in Madrid is a little strange because, well, it is, but if you are looking for a break from paella and flamenco, this festival offers you the chance to really understand this traditional Portuguese style of music. The festival is, of course, filled up with many concerts, but you can also find workshops and activities that involve the whole family during the Fado Festival, which takes place each June.

78. Visit the King of Spain's Home!

Located just 45 minutes outside of the city, the town of Aranjuez is well worth the day trip, and for one good reason – it's here that you'll find the Royal Palace of Aranjuez, which happens to be the official residence of the King of Spain. The building was completed in the mid 18th century under the reign of Philip II, and the gardens are just as impressive and expensive as the palace buildings. The palace also plays host to a museum that details the daily life of a Spanish monarch.

79. Enjoy an Afternoon Aperitif at La Ardosa

Walking past Bodega La Ardosa, you can't help but realise that you are in Madrid. Opened in 1892, this Madrid favourite still has the same old fashioned exterior, and stepping into the bar is truly like stepping back in time. The wood panelled bar is packed on weekend evenings, but come here of a weekday afternoon for a small aperitif and you can take in the whole atmosphere without jostling for bar space. And be sure to order the salmorejo (cold tomato and bread soup) – it's phenomenal.

80. Learn to Dance Like a Local at a Flamenco Class

One of the most iconic images associated with Madrid and Spain is a woman with dark hair, in a long flowing red dress, with her hands in the air dancing the famous flamenco of the country. There are plenty of flamenco performances to catch all over the city, but why not put your best foot forward and try out some flamenco moves yourself? Amor de Dios is one of the most respected flamenco schools in the city, and it caters to all levels.

81. Allow Your Jaw to Drop at the Almudena Cathedral

There is no shortage of breath taking religious architecture in the Spanish capital, and one of the most impressive churches is the Almudena Cathedral, built in the 19th century. The huge amount of space in front of the church means that you can really take in its full beauty. The interior is surprisingly modern and it even has some "pop art" elements, making this a church that is incredibly unique. In 2004, the marriage of the King, then the Prince, took place in the church, and it's a special place for many Spaniards.

82. Make Friends at a Bilingual Pub Quiz

If you're travelling to Madrid alone and your Spanish is a little bit sketchy, it can be hard to know how to make friends, and simply have a nice conversation with other people. The solution is the weekly bilingual pub quiz, "Beerlingual", which takes place every Thursday night at La Morena Cantina. The quizmasters will put you together with people of a similar language ability so that you can chat away all evening, share a few beers and plates of tapas, and impress with your general knowledge.

83. Go Shoe Shopping in Chueca

Are designer shoes your passion, perhaps even your addiction? If so, the stores of Madrid are soon going to become your best friends. But before you totally max out your credit card on your Madrid trip, you should be aware that Calle Augosto Figueroa in the centre of the trendy Chueca district is lined with discount show outlets. You'll be able to find designer names at incredible prices. Just be warned, you might have to upgrade your luggage capacity for your return journey.

84. Smell the Roses in La Roselada

Do you wish that you could take more time out to enjoy the simple things in life, like smelling a bouquet of roses? Well, Madrid offers you exactly that opportunity in the beautiful La Roselada rose garden. There are more than 500 species of roses to be explore in the garden, some Spanish, and some imported from around the globe. May and June is the best time to visit the garden, when the roses are fully in bloom and their sweet smell fills up the whole outdoor space.

85. Chow Down at Mercado San Fernando

There are numerous food markets to be explored in Madrid, but if you want to sample some delicious local treats while avoiding tourists, this is easier said than done. Mercado San Fernando is the solution, a food market that is little known to tourists, but that offers all manner of scrumptious fare. The empanadas on offer are particularly delicious, and this is also a wonderful spot to sit and relax with a pastry and a cup of coffee.

86. Watch an Old Movie in Cine Dore

Cine Dore is a Madrid institution, but it's not a place that is on the radar of most visitors to Madrid, and that makes it the perfect place to have a few hours to yourself. This cinema opened in the early 20th century, and it mostly screens old, classic movies, always in their original language with Spanish subtitles (so you don't have to worry about Spanish dubbing if your language skills aren't up to scratch). There are plush, comfy, velvet seats, and instead of the standard popcorn, you can munch on Spanish tortilla and other local comfort foods while you watch the movie.

87. Enjoy a Mellow Jazz Night at Clamores

If you've partied til you can party no more on your trip to Madrid, it might be time to slow things down a notch with a night of smooth jazz. Clamores is the ultimate place for jazz lovers in the city, with dim lighting and live music every single night of the week. You might also catch some local flamenco singing, so check out their programme to catch something that you'll enjoy.

88. Go Ham Crazy at Museo del Jamon

While in Madrid, you'll want to put as much food in your mouth as humanly possible, and the hams and cured meats are a definite highlight. Museo del Jamon is something of a Madrid institution, and tourists are often taken by the sight of the multiple cured hams hanging from the ceilings. If you are a cinema fan, you may even recognise this sight from the Almodovar movie, Live Flesh. Prices start at a very reasonable 2.50 euros for a simple ham roll, but we have the feeling that you'll be sticking around and sampling a lot more. Their sangria is also delicious!

89. Take a Crash Course in Sherry Tasting

Tucked away in the corner of the famous Mercado de San Miguel is a stall dedicated to sherry, a sweet fortified wine made from white grapes, much of which is produced in Spain. At The Sherry Corner, you are invited to take a crash course in sherry tasting. You'll get to sample six different glasses of sherry, each will be matched with a different tapa, and the whole thing costs just 25 euros. Warning: you may not want to plan any strenuous activities after your six glasses!

90. Party While Finding a Bargain at Rave Market

Madrid has an exceptional market culture, and one of the most original markets in the city is Rave Market. Is it a rave or is it a market? Well, actually it's both. This market is held every month, and the location is usually in one of Madrid's wonderful concert venues. People are also encouraged to bring their own unwanted or used items and sell them – and all while dancing to pumping tunes from the DJ booth.

91. Raise Your Adrenaline at the Parque de Attractiones

If you are the kind of person who likes to do things and be active on trips away, you might want to skip the fifth museum of the day and head to the Parque de Attraciones instead. Whether you have kids or you're a big kid yourself, this is the place to spend all day on rollercoasters, waltzers, and other fairground attractions. If you are a real daredevil, head straight for the Tornado, an upside down roller coaster that will send you zooming through the Spanish sky at 80 km/hour.

92. Fill Your Stomach at a Street Food Park

There's no shortage of great eats in Madrid, but the foodie scene tends to revolve around bar snacks and restaurant meals rather than bites you can eat on the street. There is, however one place in Madrid that is dedicated to the delights of street food – MadrEAT. Some of the food you'll be able to find from the trucks at MadrEAT include Chilean sandwiches, craft beers from Madrid, American-Asian fusion food, and French crepes.

93. Tour the Royal Tapestry Workshop

The Royal Tapestry Factory was commissioned by Philip V and opened its doors in 1720, meaning that it's almost 300 years of age. In the 18th century, a huge number of luxury goods were produced here, and the workshop is still active today, producing tapestries and carpets. The Spanish government, the Spanish Royal family, and the Vatican have all been patrons of the factory at one time or another, and Goya even started his early career here before becoming a world famous painter.

94. Drink at Madrid's Oldest Cocktail Bar

Museo Chicote is more than just a place to grab a drink, it's a place to soak in some of Madrid's drinking history as this is the oldest cocktail bar in the whole of the Spanish capital. This bar opened in 1931, and since then it has been frequented by legends such as Ernest Hemingway, Frank Sinatra, Grace Kelly, and Ava Gardner. Museo Chicote has retained its smoky, lounge atmosphere that has made it so appealing throughout the years, and there are more than 100 cocktails to try on the menu.

95. Embrace Your Inner Bookworm at the National Library

The Bibiloteca Nacional is one of the most important and beautiful buildings in Madrid. It is now over 300 years old, and it's the largest library in Spain, and one of the largest in the whole world. A visit here is a bibliophile's dream. There are interactive displays about the Spanish printing presses, illuminated manuscripts, and literary cafes inside the building where you can relax with a cup of coffee and a great book.

96. Feel the Sand Between Your Toes

As an inland city, something that Madrid does not have is a beach. If you are a beach baby and you love nothing more than to feel the sand between your toes, something you can do is head to Restaurant Ojala. They have turned their whole lower floor into a beach haven. Tonnes of sand has been brought in from the coast, and it totally covers the floor. You are encouraged to take your shoes off, kick back, and enjoy the feel of the sand beneath you.

97. Eat Cake Made by Nuns!

It's not every day that you have the opportunity to buy cookies and cakes made by the fair hands of nuns. But in Madrid anything is possible. At the Corpus Christi Convent, which happens to be a beautiful building, the nuns make a little sideline of income for the convent by baking up a storm in the convent kitchen. You are welcome to pop in and buy a delicious treat. It's sure to be the holiest slice of cake you'll ever consume.

98. Say Hey to the Spanish Tooth Fairy

In Spain, instead of having a tooth fairy that takes away a young child's baby teeth, they have a tooth rat who is named Raton Perez. Well, believe it or not, there is a whole museum dedicated to this little rodent in Madrid. If you have some spare time to fill, pop in and learn about the story of his life and visit his home inside a biscuit tin.

99. Eat Japanese Food in a War Bunker

So, you probably haven't booked a trip to Madrid to eat Japanese food, but the Yugo The Bunker restaurant is something a little different – the whole place has been designed to look exactly like a Japanese war bunker, so if you enjoy war atrocities with your sushi, this is the place to chow down. Novelty aside, the food is actually really good. All the sushi items like temaki and niguiri are stellar, but it's the kobe beef that really steals the show.

100. Stock Up on Violet Candies

Savoury dishes are certainly more famous than sweets when it comes to Madrid's culinary culture, but if you have a sweet tooth, you won't want to miss out on the violet candies that are the typical sweet treat of the capital. There is one place and one place only to stock up on your candies, and that's a small shop with a wooden façade called La Violeta, which has been open since 1915. There are other sweets here too, but the violet candies are the specialty.

101. Have a Purse or Satchel Specially Made

In the historic centre of the city lies Taller Puntera, a workshop space that specialises in the production of hand crafted leather goods. You can simply buy one of their beautiful items off the shelf of the shop floor, but if you have a little bit more time, you can actually have something specially made. The artisans will talk you through all the options, from colours to shapes, sizes to the softness of the leather. Can you think of a better memory to home from your trip?

Before You Go...

Hey you! Thanks so much for reading **101 Coolest Things to Do in Madrid**. We really hope that this helps to make your time in Madrid the most fun and memorable trip that it can be. And if you enjoyed reading the book, it would be super cool if you could leave a review on the book's Amazon web page. Thanks so much!

Keep your eyes peeled on **www.101coolestthings.com** and **keep it cool!**